STEP UP
TO THE MIC

STEP UP TO THE MIC

A Positive Approach to Succeeding in Voice-Overs

RODNEY SAULSBERRY
VISUAL & PERFORMING ARTS

TOMDOR PUBLISHING
Agoura Hills, Calif.

Published by Tomdor Publishing, LLC
P.O. Box 1735 Agoura Hills, CA 91376-1735
Tel: 818-207-2682 Fax: 818-707-8591
www.tomdorpublishing.com

PUBLISHER'S CATALOGING-IN-PUBLICATION DATA
Saulsberry, Rodney.

Step up to the mic: a positive approach to succeeding in voice-overs/ Rodney Saulsberry—Agoura Hills, Calif.: Tomdor Publishing, 2007.

p. ; cm.
ISBN-13:978-0-9747678-9-5
ISBN-10: 0-9747678-9-1
Includes bibliographical references.

1. Voice actors and actresses. 2. Voice-overs—Vocational guidance. 3. Television announcing—Vocational guidance. 4. Radio announcing—Vocational guidance. 5. Success. 6. Self-actualization (Psychology). I. Title.

PN1990.9.A54 S28 2007   2006926753
792.02/8/023—dc22   0612

Printed in the United States of America

Cover design by Kristine Mills-Knoble
Copyediting and book design by Mary Jo Zazueta
Back cover photography by Carrie Cavalier
Illustrations by Todd James

To my mother, Dorothy Jane.
You inspire me.
I love you.

Contents

CONTENTS

SECTION III:
INSPIRATIONAL & MOTIVATIONAL CONTRIBUTIONS

Foreword

I FIRST MET RODNEY IN A SMALL SOUND BOOTH when I was auditioning actors for Adult Swim's *Minoriteam* animated series. Rodney was the first person I interviewed for the role of Fasto. After Rodney did just one read I realized I didn't need to see anyone else.

It's rare that someone comes in and nails the part immediately, but Rodney is a singular talent. More importantly, he has the mark of a true professional. He comes into every voice-over session with a positive attitude, great ideas, and an open mind. When he steps up to the mic, he's not just ready to work, he's ready to help create a character.

Listen to what this man has to say. He knows what he is talking about, and he's writing it down for you to use. There is no greater gift.

— Adam de la Peña
Executive Producer, *Minoriteam*

Preface

WHEN YOU ARE ASKED WHAT PLEASES you most in life, your response is most likely swift, precise, and to the point. You don't have to search for superlatives to describe what you are most passionate about. The words flow from your lips like raindrops nourishing the pasture of your passion.

Those of us who are part of the voice-over industry speak in this manner all the time, because we truly love what we do. We have the dream jobs—the opportunity to use our vocal gifts to promote products and causes we believe in, and to give voice to animated characters that entertain our children, while encouraging them to grow up and use their voices to bring joy to others.

As much as you love what you do, there will be times when you do not work steadily and you might question your decision to pursue this career. I wrote this book to help you through those challenging periods.

Step Up to the Mic is a feel-good book that reminds you of the power of positive thinking. The abil-

ity to put your career on a pathway to financial and
spiritual success is within your power. Affirmation of
your worth is available 24/7—if you want it.

You don't have to go far to get this affirmation,
because it is within you. The choice is yours. You can
sit around and fret, or you can get up and smile. Feel
grateful for good health and spiritual prosperity as you
pursue your goals.

Once you lift the burden of negativity off your
back, you acquire clarity. Your mind is now free to think
and be creative. Doors that were shut suddenly open
wide. Concepts that were too complicated to conceive,
become crystal clear.

Not only will I teach you how to channel positive
thinking into your everyday existence, I will point you
in the direction of classes, books, and life lessons that
will help you flourish.

When you erase the self-doubt, you build the
ladder to self-confidence and success! It's time to get
busy. It's time to *Step Up to the Mic*!

Acknowledgments

I GRATEFULLY ACKNOWLEDGE MY ENTIRE FAMILY, AS well as my friends, students, and everyone who contributed to the making of this book. I sincerely love and thank you all.

STEP UP
TO THE MIC

How to Use This Book

THERE ARE MANY VOICE-OVER BOOKS ON THE market that tell you how to make a demo, find an agent, market yourself, etc. This book tells you how to go about those activities—and more—in the right frame of mind.

Step Up to the Mic is an uplifting handbook, for both the novice and the seasoned pro, as you go about your daily job of trying to be successful in the voice-over business.

The information in these pages will aid you emotionally, spiritually, and physically every day. The positive affirmations and exercises will provide you with the ammunition you need to deal with your employers, competition, and colleagues.

You should study the concepts weekly—if not daily—until they become a part of your life, fabric, and philosophy. Keep this book with you at all times and refer to it in job situations when you need a reminder of the positive power that you possess inside.

Do the positive exercises for at least ten minutes a day when needed, and watch your goals become realities in a relatively short period of time. This is not a book to be read and put away. You should read it over and over again. Refer to it not only in tough times, but also in good times, to make a positive thing even better.

SECTION I

FINDING YOUR POSITIVE ATTITUDE

CHAPTER 1

Why a Positive Attitude Is Necessary

B Y DECIDING TO BECOME A VOICE-OVER ACTOR, you have chosen to be part of an exciting industry. However, you have also entered a highly competitive field. Every day in your voice-over career, you will encounter obstacles that challenge your talent, your patience, and your interpersonal skills. In this book, I teach you positive ways to meet those challenges head-on.

To begin, we will explore why a positive attitude is necessary in a voice-over career. It's all about competition. Every time you audition, you're competing with somebody else. But, every time you step into the recording booth to lay down a track, you're competing with yourself. Sometimes this competition can feel like mental warfare. (I'll explain that idea shortly.)

First, let's talk about competition with other performers. Voice-over is a national phenomenon, and it seems everybody wants to be a part of it. Here are some of the reasons why:

○ It doesn't matter what you look like.

○ It doesn't matter how old you are.

○ There is plenty of residual income.

○ You can work from home.

○ All you need is talent.

○ All you have to do is believe in yourself.

So if anybody can be a voice-over artist, how can you push yourself to be a better voice-over artist? By winning the struggle of mental warfare.

. . . if you make a positive attitude the center of your identity, your life will become more positive as a result.

Mental Warfare

The battle between your positive and negative mental energy dictates how your day will be. If you let the negative energy win, you will fail in everything you attempt to do on a given day.

I will teach you how to fight the daily battle and how to win the constant war.

Let's call the combatants in this mental warfare your positive and negative inner voices. You create your reality by what you think and perceive in your mind. Therefore, if you make a positive attitude the center of your identity, your life will become more positive as a result. When you establish a positive attitude at the center of your constitution, you will possess the most powerful weapon in the world, and your life and career will flourish abundantly.

When you establish a positive attitude at the center of your constitution, you will possess the most powerful weapon in the world . . .

Following is a simple exercise to fight those negative demons that can consume your everyday thoughts. Whenever they pop up in your mind, fight the negative words (see the list on the left) with positive words (see the list on the right). Go through this exercise whenever you feel the need.

Replace negative words . . .	with positive words:
No . . .	Yes
You can't . . .	I can
You will never find work . . .	I will always work
You can do it tomorrow . . .	I will do it today
You're not good enough . . .	I'm the best that I can be

Sooner, rather than later, you must stop spending

energy on negative words and thoughts. Repeat the positive affirmations on the right as many times as you need to each day.

The Benefits of a Positive Attitude

A positive attitude can help you face and surmount the challenges you will encounter in your voice-over career. Here are some of the benefits of having a positive attitude:

○ Achieving your goals

○ Avoiding self-sabotage

○ Feeling less stress

○ Achieving success faster and more easily

○ Being happier

○ Having more energy

○ Having greater inner power and strength

○ Being able to inspire and motivate yourself

○ Being able to overcome any difficulty

Your positive attitude expresses itself in the following ways:

○ Optimism

○ Positive thinking

○ Creative thinking

○ Expecting great success

○ Embracing others

○ Being inspired

○ Never giving up

○ Looking at problems as blessings in disguise

○ Displaying self-esteem and confidence

○ Seeing opportunities

You can develop a positive attitude by choosing to look at the brighter side of life all the time. It's really that simple.

Choose to be happy instead of sad. Find reasons to smile more often. Read books that inspire you and make you feel good. If you learn to master your thoughts, you can channel positive energy into every aspect of your life.

By having a positive attitude, you can earn more money, take your career to new heights, and achieve your goals.

YOU SHOULD LOVE YOUR WORK

You don't become successful at
anything if you just like it.
You have to love it.

CHAPTER 2

Build a
Positive Foundation

I KNOW WHAT YOU'RE THINKING. YOU'RE THINKING it's easy for me to talk about *having* a positive attitude because I'm a successful voice-over artist. Well, guess what? I attained success by having a positive attitude. In other words, finding my positive attitude helped me find success.

You can do the same—if you train yourself to avoid negative thoughts. I call this building a positive foundation. Let's get started.

> "Happiness is something that you are and it comes from the way you think."
>
> ~ WAYNE DYER

Get the Right Voice-Over Nutrients

Just like you need to ingest proper nutrients to stay healthy physically, you also need positive nutrients to develop, nourish, stimulate, and maintain a healthy mind. These positive nutrients will sustain you in good and bad times during your career.

Here are some ways to add nutrients to your voice-over program:

Put Together a Team

○ Find an agent you believe in, and who believes in you.

○ Get a financial advisor you trust to advise you and take good care of your money.

○ Interact with friends who stimulate you in a positive way.

○ Get rid of people in your life who bring you down.

○ Find your signature voice, and stop trying to excel in areas that don't suit your talent.

○ Elevate your game.

Once you have purged some of the negativity that stops you from being successful and added positive nutrients, you can set higher goals, face new challenges, and work harder than you ever have before.

CHAPTER 3

A Positive Attitude Is Spiritual

FAITH HAS BEEN AND IS IMPORTANT IN MY LIFE and career, so I always spread the message to people who will listen. When you read this chapter, keep in mind that faith can be anything you want it to be. I have faith, an unwavering belief that I will succeed at whatever endeavor I choose.

Being a Christian helps me stay strong and positive. Find out what gives you inner strength, and draw on that when you're developing your positive attitude.

You may not believe that spirituality plays a part in a successful voice-over career, but I'm here to tell you it does.

Your Inner Spirit

You are the embodiment of many powers, and the main source of these powers is your inner spirit. These powers increase when you are completely in touch with your inner consciousness. When you believe you have the power to create monetary success, physical health, joy, and persisting peace, you will experience a sense of victory that powers you through the everyday obstacles in the voice-over industry.

It is this inner spirit that allows you to succeed on a day-to-day basis. What you show to others on the exterior is manufactured by your inner spirit. It's hard to be content on the outside if you don't have your inside together.

> When you believe you have the power to create monetary success, physical health, joy, and persisting peace, you will experience a sense of victory that powers you through the everyday obstacles in the voice-over industry.

What's going on with your body? Do you feel nauseous? Do you have a headache? What about an ulcer? There is a medical remedy for each of these ailments, but the remedy for your inner spirit can't be purchased at a pharmacy. Your inner spirit is controlled, processed, and healed by you and only you.

The term "butterflies in the stomach" describes the nervousness and sense of unease that can overcome you when you are faced with a task you could either perform successfully or fail completely. This uneasy feeling is your inner spirit at work.

> When you approach a piece of voice-over copy that is outside your comfort zone, the challenge to make the words your own is presented to your inner spirit.

I always welcome butterflies because they put me on my toes. Nine times out of ten, I complete tasks successfully because of this high state of alertness. My inner spirit propels me to outrageous heights that surprise me—and others who observe my success.

When you approach a piece of voice-over copy that is outside your comfort zone, the challenge to make the words your own is presented to your inner spirit. Believe that your inner spirit will provide you the strength to succeed.

Once you have acquired the ability to fashion your thoughts and emotions in a positive way, you will be able to conquer the worst situations that arise. Nothing external or internal can defeat you when you recognize the power of your inner spirit. You will not be affected by negative circumstances that confront you, rather you will turn negatives into positives—and take total control of the situation. With this power you can alleviate stress, pain, and anxiety.

Accept Your Abundance

Remember the saying "Every dog has his day"? Well, one day you will be very successful in this business. I know you will, because you have toiled long and hard perfecting your craft. You took classes. You took care of yourself physically, and you were good to your fellow man.

For those of you who are already successful, keep doing what you're doing; obviously it's working.

Oftentimes though, we don't know how to accept abundance when we get it. In some cases, we don't feel worthy. Don't be alarmed. You're not unique if you feel uncomfortable about receiving good fortune.

The first thing you need to do is realize that you deserve all that is happening to you. The hard work that you put in is finally paying off. Don't feel guilty. Revel in your success and invest your abundance wisely.

Abundance is not always monetary or material. You can acquire an abundance of confidence, courage, or love from others. You have to be able to accept those blessings, too. Abundance is prosperity.

Don't feel guilty. Revel in your success
and invest your abundance wisely.

Here is a list of prosperity affirmations that you can refer to whenever you feel guilty or ashamed of receiving the fruits of your labor in abundance.

○ I release my fear of wealth.

○ There is a limitless supply of voice-over opportunity, and it is mine.

○ I open myself to receive the abundance of the voice-over universe.

○ I allow myself to prosper in the entertainment industry.

○ I am not afraid to be successful.

Spiritual Connections

No matter what your religious affiliation is, you can't deny the spiritual aspect of the phenomenon of human life. Everything around you is a miracle to behold—including your voice-over career.

Everything around you is a miracle
to behold—including your
voice-over career.

How do you explain that you auditioned and booked a job on the day your throat was so sore from the common cold that you could barely speak? Somehow, your audition was good enough to get you the biggest moneymaking commercial in your entire career. What do you attribute your good fortune to? Luck? Happenstance?

I give credit to God almighty. I have a God con-

CREATE VOICE-OVER WEALTH

Build your own reality pyramid by visualizing your financial success.

sciousness. Through my Christian faith and constant prayer, I have made it my business to know who is responsible for my success.

Consider these words from Galatians [6:4&5]:

"Make a careful exploration of who you are and the work you have been given, and then sink yourself into that. Don't be impressed with yourself. Don't compare yourself with others. Each of you must take responsibility for doing the creative best you can with your own life."

CHAPTER 4

A Positive Approach to Voice-Over Work

I N MY FIRST BOOK, *YOU CAN BANK ON YOUR VOICE*, I shared my knowledge of how to produce a demo, find an agent, and excel at auditions. Now I will go a little deeper and show you how to pursue these things in a positive way.

Making a Demo

The voice-over business has changed drastically in recent years when it comes to making a voice-over demo. The length of the presentation is much shorter— a maximum of ninety-five seconds—therefore, demos have less content. And the focus is not just on the sound of your voice but also on the natural, easy delivery that must be apparent from the first words you speak.

Packaging is still important, but the ability to send your demo to agents and prospective employers via the Internet is crucial in this cyberspace age. These changes are easy to adjust to. All you have to do is accept them and—with a sense of positive purpose—make your demo.

When you approach this project with an open and free mind, you will create an environment that allows you to excel and produce a quality demo.

The packaging should be simple, smart, and tidy—keeping the expense to a minimum. Limit your first run to however many CDs you need to cover the contacts you have researched and deemed worthy to receive a copy of your demo.

When you approach this project with an open and free mind, you will create an environment that allows you to excel and produce a quality demo.

Auditioning

Stop making the auditioning process such a painful experience. Look at it as an opportunity to get work. Getting work is a positive thing, so why do you make the pursuit of work so negative?

Starting today, embrace the challenge of impressing directors and producers. You should believe that the worst thing about your situation is that you don't have ten more auditions lined up right after this one.

Look forward to auditions like you do your favorite holiday, because auditions truly are special occasions—if you choose to see them that way.

With a positive attitude, you can claim the voice-over career that you deserve. As soon as you conquer your fear of casting directors, everything about the auditioning process will change for you. Respect them, but don't put casting directors on pedestals. They breathe and bleed just like you do. They are human beings, no better and no worse than you.

> With a positive attitude, you can claim the voice-over career that you deserve.

If you do good work, they're in your corner—because when you perform well, you make them look good to their employers. It's a win-win situation.

A little nervous energy is okay, but the minute you assume that deer-in-the-headlights position, you stick out like a sore thumb. Directors detect fear quickly, which makes your audition an uphill battle that you can't possibly win.

Therefore, think positive, and you will act and move with a confident gait that seeps into your performance and makes you nothing short of magnificent in your delivery and intent.

THAT PRIZE

The sea of bodies filled the hall
As I set foot on the grounds of a cattle call
Struggled to find that private place
Where I could practice out loud, proud with pace
Slow, then fast, then slow again
Took a peek at my watch for my time to go in
To that scary room with my script in my hand
Prepared to do whatever, however they demand
One read, that's all, so back into the hall
Where others look into my eyes
And struggle to see if I left that prize
Is the job still free? I heard somebody say.
I see them all wither, cause they know deep inside
I claimed that audition! I took that prize!

—*Rodney Saulsberry*

Then, if the director asks for more takes, he or she will do so from a position of respect and camaraderie, because you and the director have become partners in pursuit of a great audition.

Never fear the person or persons you are auditioning for. You are equals, and you're all after the same thing: excellence.

Once you accept the concept of feeling good about yourself, others will join you in that assessment.

Finding an Agent

Why would anyone want to represent me? That is the first question to ask yourself. Take out a pen and some paper, and write down why you are worthy of representation. There should be many good reasons on that list: talent, perseverance, patience, love for yourself, etc.

Yes, you read that right. You have to love yourself—and your talent—to succeed in the voice-over business.

If you walk into any agent's office with those qualities, you'll have your pick of suitors who want to help you succeed. Those qualities will also manifest in the demos you submit to agents over the Internet and through the mail. Once you accept the concept of feeling good about yourself, others will join you in that assessment.

Reading Copy

The key to successfully choosing how to interpret a piece of commercial copy is to trust yourself. If you are a seasoned professional, years of experience have given

RADIATE
CONFIDENCE DAILY

Project a face of supreme
confidence when you work
and when you audition.

you the ability to make good interpretation choices. If you are a novice, reading books and taking classes can give you the same ability.

Learn to trust yourself.

Believe in yourself.

If you know in your heart that you have put in the work to learn how to interpret copy, your choices are trustworthy.

INTERPRETATION

Earphones on my head, every word that I said

Returned to my ear transfix

Got a certain amount of time to let it rip and unwind

The words travel from my mouth to the mix

Who said "Read it this way"?

Who said "Do it like that"?

I got my own *interpretation* and I think it's *phat*!

Top of the line is the microphone, I'm rockin

My own version of the text is the theme I'm poppin

The VO direction means nothing to me

I'm doin' it my way for the world to see

Cause it's not about the sound or the new sensation

Cause it's not about the intent or the writer's fixation

It's about how I feel—and my *interpretation*

—*Rodney Saulsberry*

Working With Other Talent

You work in a highly competitive community, but there's a positive way to compete and work with other voice-over performers. Be courteous and respectful to your fellow artists. Learn to give everyone at the audition, as well as on the job, the benefit of the doubt when they do something that may seem rude or deceitful. Sometimes nervous energy causes people to act out of character and forget to be respectful. Don't let another person's shortcomings drag you down to his or her level.

Avoid the drama, and claim the positive energy in the room.

Give Praise to Those Around You

Your sessions can be a haven of joy if you use positive reinforcement when relating to the people with whom you work. This behavior will more often than not bring about positive consequences; that is the more sweetness you give out, the more sweetness you will receive.

Take the time to praise the engineer and the director. You can even compliment the other talent in the session, when it's appropriate to do so. Some people call this bribery or flattery. Maybe it is, but the purpose of this behavior is to make the workplace a happy and joyous environment for everyone.

Be sincere in your praise, not forced. If you deliver it when it is warranted, it will not come off as fake.

I'm not asking you to be a kiss-ass—just suggesting that if you're nice to others, they will be nice to you.

Onward and Upward

At this point, you should get the message: adopting a positive attitude affects every aspect of your voice-over career. Section One gave you tools to find the positive attitude that works for you. In Section Two, we'll discuss how to use your positive attitude in your voice-over work.

SECTION II

USING YOUR
POSITIVE ATTITUDE

CHAPTER 5

Overcoming Obstacles

E VERY PROFESSION HAS CHALLENGES, AND VOICE-OVER work is no different. In the next few chapters, I'll talk about some positive ways you can overcome challenges in the workplace and throughout your voice-over career. Let's start with obstacles we all face every day.

Obstacle #1: Procrastination

I'm not going to beat you up and tell you how unfortunate it is that you haven't made a voice-over demo yet. Or harass you about the five hundred copies of your demo that are sitting in a box out in your garage.

Do these scenarios sound familiar? Have I reached you yet? Are you a procrastinator? Well, there's good news: it's never too late to change. You can still make good on the promise you made to yourself to be successful in this competitive field, today!

Eventually the things you are truly passionate about get done. If you continue to put something off, you probably don't want to do it. Say ten years have passed, and you still haven't taken the initial steps to pursue your so-called passion. Maybe you're not as passionate about this business as you thought.

But, if you are passionate about voice-over as a career, stop putting things off. Stop procrastinating.

The key to going after your goals is to make them seem achievable.

I hear you—"I'll get to it someday." Well, someday is not on the calendar. You have Monday, Tuesday, Wednesday, Thursday, Friday, Saturday, and Sunday—but *someday* is not an option.

The key to going after your goals is to make them seem achievable. Okay, your dreams are huge—simply divide them into smaller pieces so that the task of reaching them doesn't appear insurmountable.

For example, if you want to be the promo voice for the ABC network, start by trying to become the voice of an ABC affiliate first. If your goal is to be with the biggest voice-over agency in the industry, start by signing with a smaller agency first. You're more likely to put off chasing your big dreams if you don't think you can make them come true. Realistic goals are more appealing and more likely to be reached. Here are two exercises to help you stop procrastinating.

Exercise A. Let's break down a big goal into something that only takes a few minutes to work on. The goal is putting together your home studio. Write down your assignment: "Search the Internet for information on home studios for 15 minutes three times a week." That's a good start. The hardest thing to do is to start a project, so this exercise will at least get you on your way.

Exercise B. Write your goals on postcards and tape a card to your bathroom mirror, on a wall near the towel rack in your bathroom, and on the refrigerator door. When the postcards remind you about something you have put off, the chances of you pursuing those goals are greatly improved.

Obstacle #2: Rejection

The remedy to rejection is to have many irons in the fire at one time. In other words, you need to get a lot of auditions so that you are not unbalanced or overly concerned about any one of them.

Rejection is hard to cope with. I have often complained about not getting a particular job. And I sometimes get distressed when a commercial campaign I auditioned for turns out to be a major hit and I have to listen to the spot every day being voiced by another actor. (A fellow actor once told me: "If you don't want to hear the spot, change the channel when that spot comes on." Good advice.)

Don't take rejection personally. You really didn't get rejected—you just didn't get the job.

MOVE ON

When you don't get a job that you auditioned for, don't stress about it. Move on to the next audition.

Obstacle #3: Illness/Problems at Home

Whenever you're not feeling well or there are problems at home, you need to put those things behind you before you show up at work. To deliver a good voice-over performance, you need a clear head.

Whenever I want to focus on an assignment, I tell myself "I'm on the job." That's a very positive thing for me—I'm working, and I love what I do. But everyone has their own way to get past problems that can affect their performance.

Here are some ideas that might work for you:

○ If you've had a fight with your spouse or you're having emotional problems with your family, you must absorb yourself in the work environment once you get to the job. Concentrate on the environment you're in and totally forget about the outside world or any-thing else that is happening in your life.

○ Engross yourself in the script and in the people in the room. In your head, say: "These people are my family for the duration of the session." That way, they become the most important people in your world, until the work is done.

○ If a part of your body aches, before you start to read your copy, say: "My body feels great."

○ Mentally change who you are and how you feel and the atmosphere will become con-ducive to achieving a top-notch performance. You can do it!

○ Pretend that the session is all that your life is about, then you'll be able to engross yourself in the situation.

○ Say to yourself: "I'm not dealing with the future; I'm not dealing with the past. I'm acting in the present."

○ If you come to the job with baggage, get rid of the baggage by saying: "I am only dealing with what's happening to me right now."

Obstacle #4: Difficult Copy

The positive way to deal with copy that's hard to say is: take your time.

If I look at copy and realize it's challenging, I know I'll have to concentrate. I spot words that might be tough, and then I go over them a number of times in my mind—and aloud if I can—so that when I get to them during a take, I don't stumble.

If a small portion of the copy is really crazy, I will say so to the employer—in a polite way. If the writer happens to be there, then I'll try to be tactful by saying "Well, this is a little hard to say."

Sometimes I will read the copy slightly differently than how it's written without asking if I can. Many times when this happens, the client or director will comment, "You know, you did *this* where I had *that*, but to be honest with you, I really liked what you were doing. Can you do it again?" Nine times out of ten, you won't have to alter the script anyway. Professional ad writers are generally excellent at their work.

Before you suggest a change, try saying the difficult copy first. Asking to change the script should be a last resort, and you always have to be tactful about it.

Remember, everyone in the room has the same positive goal—you all want to do a great job.

Obstacle #5: They Keep Changing the Copy

The flip side to difficult copy is copy that keeps changing. It is a tough situation when a client can't decide what words he or she wants you to record. Here are some ways to keep your cool when this happens.

- ○ Keep a positive attitude when there are copy changes during a session by realizing that oftentimes copywriters aren't sure, or they are on deadline, or they have to turn in copy before they are ready. Sometimes they will be writing copy while you're working.

- ○ Remember, you could be doing something else that you don't like as much. Voice-over is fun!

- ○ Remember that these people have brought you here—they are paying you a certain amount of money, and there is a certain amount of time they have with you contractually. It's their time, and they can use it how they want.

- ○ Understand that when people are in the creative process, sometimes things change. Just put on a positive hat that says: "They are in the creative process and they are under the gun. I'm here to do a job, and I will do it."

Obstacle #6: Switching Character Voices

Remember you have your main voice—your signature voice. Most of the time, that's what employers want you to use. Even if you go into a high falsetto or if you go into a low basso thing, it still has an origin, and that origin is your signature voice.

Therefore, even if you play a character with a unique voice, you're really doing a variation of what's already there. This knowledge comes in handy when you're asked to play more than one character during a session.

When you work in a cartoon, you have your main role, though contractually you may have to do two, three, or four other minor characters. If this is the case, you have to say to yourself, "Okay, the main character I'm doing is about up here," meaning your voice is at a particular high pitch. Then, you've got to take the next character into a lower voice. If the higher guy spoke rapidly, the lower guy might speak more slowly and deliberately.

Obstacle #7: Offensive Copy

There will be times when you are given copy that you're not excited about morally. It may insult you as a female or an ethnic minority, or it may be against your religious or personal beliefs. What do you do?

You tell the client or director that it offends you, and explain why. Ask them to change the copy, and hope for the best.

When I've had jobs where the text has been offensive and I have taken the time to alert the director, for the most part, we have had a civil dialogue about it, and the changes were made.

One thing about the voice-over industry is that it's a friendly community. I think the reason I love it is because it's generally a happy environment. So, when things really bother you, your employers are usually open for discussion.

The last thing I will say on this subject is that my advice deals with situations where you get to a job and encounter offensive copy *you never saw before*. If the copy bothered you during an audition, you shouldn't have taken the job.

There's nothing more empowering than avoiding a situation that could be a problem before it actually becomes a problem.

Obstacle #8: Casting Errors

Sometimes you get into situations where you're working the job and you realize that the client has made a mistake. You don't know if they cast the wrong voice-over actor or what, but you're there and it's just not working for you.

Nine times out of ten, that's just your opinion. You have to trust that they have you there because they listened to your audition and thought it would work. You have to think positively and believe you can make it happen. Let the client or director determine when it's obvious you're not right for a job and the session is over.

The positive thing to do is to convince yourself that the client and director know something you don't. If they believe you're right for this part, do what you can to make their assessment correct.

Obstacle #9: Fear

No one is immune to fear; we all deal with fear in various ways. If you recognize that you are fearful of a situation, person, place, or thing, you are headed in the right direction; now you can work on getting rid of that fear.

First you need to rationalize the worthiness of what you fear. Ask yourself, is this really worth fearing? Is it a matter of life or death? How does this rate with the important things in my world? Is it high or low on my importance chart?

> "Whatever you fear most has no power—it is your fear that has the power."
>
> —OPRAH WINFREY

The answer to these questions should put your fear in its proper perspective. After going through this exercise, if you still can't defeat your fear, you will probably have to take more desperate measures, maybe even seek professional help. If, however, it was just a matter of prioritizing the importance of the fear, you can now move on.

In the voice-over workplace you might sometimes fear what others will bring to the session and audition environment. Instead of worrying about what you are going to *encounter* when you meet others, decide what you're going to *bring* to the environment to deflect whatever comes your way. I call this my "bring pack."

Make sure you always bring your bring pack to work with you, don't leave home without it.

Here are some of the contents that should be in your bring pack:

Energy to battle those who are fatigued

Hope to battle those who have despair

A *smile* to battle those who frown

Kindness to battle those who are rude

Love to battle those who hate

Patience to battle those who are restless

Joy to battle those who bring sorrow

Peace to battle those who bring war

Professionalism to battle those who act like amateurs

These concepts should make your work a little less fearful.

Obstacle #10: The Holiday Season

The entire voice-over industry shuts down completely between Christmas and New Year's. This festive season is the longest vacation period of the year and, unfortunately, things don't return to normal until the middle of January.

CHALLENGES ARE STEPPING-STONES

Don't let the obstacles in front of you keep you down. Step over them and go up to your prize.

In the past, I suffered greatly during the holidays. But, after sending e-mails and phoning other creative people in the entertainment community, I realized that they, too, shared my pain. It was just a part of the business.

When you work freelance, the last thing you want is a long unpaid vacation. Every day is a potential workday, so you don't want to forsake any of them.

Eventually, I came to terms with the hiatus and decided to use the quiet holiday season to prepare for the coming year. You should, too.

I recommend writing out your list of tasks on the day after Thanksgiving. Here are some ideas for holiday-season chores:

- ○ I will read that voice-over book I haven't had time to read.
- ○ I will map out career moves for the new year.
- ○ I will practice that dialect I always wanted to do better.
- ○ I will update my mailing list of casting directors and producers.
- ○ I will review my demos and consider redoing them.
- ○ I will consider the effectiveness of my present representation.
- ○ I will compile a list of new contacts.
- ○ I will rearrange my office and make it more conducive to success.

○ I will work on finding my signature voice.

○ I will challenge myself.

How can you challenge yourself? The "sound-alike" industry is booming these days. Very often, clients want actors that can sound like or do impressions of George Bush, Arnold Schwarzenegger, Fred Flintstone, Eddie Murphy, Will Smith, Brad Pitt, Morgan Freeman . . . you get the idea. It behooves you to learn how to sound like famous characters and people—and the holiday downtime is the perfect opportunity to do so. Producers would love to hire you over the real thing. You're a lot cheaper!

CHAPTER 6

Working With Difficult People

TO SUCCEED IN VOICE-OVER, YOU MUST LEARN to take the good with the bad. One of the toughest areas of this business is working with difficult people. Most of the professionals I encounter in voice-over work are terrific people who just want to do a good job; but sometimes people bring their baggage to work, and that adds tension to recording sessions.

Maybe the person isn't happy with his or her position in the industry. Maybe he or she is going through marital problems. Whatever—it's none of your business. Rise above it all by minding your own business, period! Your business is doing a great job and staying positive throughout the session.

Difficult Directors

Hopefully the directors you work with will instruct you in helpful ways. But if you find yourself working for a director who can't or won't offer you useful guidance, you may want to follow the advice I'm about to offer.

The way I deal with a director who gives me instructions that aren't helpful is to remind myself that everything the director says is important. That's why they call him or her the director. It is my job to please him or her. So, when a director tells me something I feel is wrong, I must first do it the way he or she wants me to do it.

I'll give you an example. Some directors want to give you a reading. A reading is when they tell you how to perform the copy by reading it aloud themselves and then asking you to mimic them. When this happens, copy their performance and their interpretation. Sometimes directors are good at this. I'll listen and say to myself, "You know, I understand that interpretation, and what they did was great. I'm going to perform it exactly that way."

Remember, you have been hired because you bring a certain style and panache to the job—but it's their time. Try hard to do what the director asks, and speak up tactfully if it becomes clear the director doesn't know what he or she wants. A positive and friendly approach to any difficult situation with a director will generally result in a peaceful resolution that is satisfactory to everyone involved.

You should always take the high road.

Your So-Called Friends

Avoid negative people, even your so-called friends who are also in the voice-over industry. Beware of your rivals. These are people who claim to be your friend—but they are silently hoping for your demise. They don't want you to get the voice-over job you have always coveted. They give you advice they know is wrong and meant to make you fail. In her book, *Fearless Living*, author Rhonda Britten describes these people as "rivals in disguise."

Beware of your rivals. These are
people who claim to be your
friend—but they are silently hoping
for your demise.

Here are some examples of what a so-called friend, coming out of an audition that you're about to go into, might say:

- ○ They loved me. I think I got it.
- ○ Don't you think Michelle Bray would be great for this?
- ○ I'll wait for you—hurry up.
- ○ Wow . . . tough room.
- ○ You can go home, I booked it.

This person considers herself a friend, but in reality, she feels threatened by you. She needs to keep you by her side so that she can keep a finger on your progress, a stopper on your career.

If you have anyone in your life who can't deal with your desire to live in a positive way, it's time for you to separate yourself from him or her.

More So-Called Friends

Do you have so-called friends, who remind you of negatives from your past with the intent to disrupt your present happiness? They hate to see you smiling, so they bring up incidents that you have forgotten about and moved on from. It's amazing how insensitive some people can be. Author Rhonda Britten calls these types "rearview mirrors."

So-called friends say things like: "I'll never forget when they replaced you on that cartoon. That was a sad day when you called me. How many seasons has it been on the air now? Do you ever talk to the guy who replaced you?"

If you have anyone in your life who can't deal with your desire to live in a positive way, it's time for you to separate yourself from him or her. If you choose to keep this person in your life, the next time he or she brings up something sad from your past, quickly switch the subject. As far as this particular friend is concerned, you have to be in total control of all conversations at all times.

Bad Attitudes

Sometimes you can't figure out why a client or a director or an engineer is making a session difficult. Maybe they prejudged you, maybe they heard gossip about you, or maybe they're just angry at the world. Getting into conflict with these people is another way of giving in to negativity. Stay positive, and you can probably remove the tension from the situation.

If someone is determined to treat you badly during the entire session, compliment him or her. Turn the tables. Whenever they throw a dagger, throw a rose.

Pretty soon the person will realize there is no combat.

Infighting

If you're in a session where two people are going at each other, for whatever reason—just be a bystander. Don't take sides.

You have to be a diplomat. I'm not telling you to avoid people, because you want to be nice to everyone, but never get into a situation where you're talking privately with a guy or girl who's not getting along with another person at the session. In some nice way, keep your distance.

Why? Let's say you go over to one of the combatants and start up a casual conversation and that actor starts unloading about why he or she is angry with the other actor. You're not doing anything wrong, but if the other actor walks by and notices you conversing with the enemy, it seems like you're participating in a conspiratorial exchange.

Keep your relationships with people who cause friction in sessions limited. Be polite. Say hello and good-bye—but avoid getting into deep conversations with them.

. . . it's important to presume that you're never off-mic. If you're in the booth, assume the people in the control room can hear you.

Also, it's important to presume that you're never off-mic. If you're in the booth, assume the people in the control room can hear you. So, when you're having dialogue that is outside of the copy you're reading, it shouldn't be political, and it shouldn't be personal. Anything outside of the weather is not safe to talk about. You never know who is listening, so stay positive and stay focused on the work. That way, no one can drag you into his or her negative situation.

CHAPTER 7

Teamwork in Voice-Over Sessions

THE FIRST STEP TO SHARING YOUR POSITIVE ATTITUDE is to be professional: arrive on time, know what's expected of you, listen to direction, make every take a great take, and don't complain or make excuses.

The second step is to be a team player. Treat the participants in a session like a baseball team, with each individual having a specific responsibility. The actor, engineer, and director have an area that they are in charge of. Problems occur when an individual steps outside of his or her area. Let's explore a common situation where voice-over artists get frustrated—even though they shouldn't.

That Wasn't My Best Take!

How do you deal with hearing the final product of

a voice-over session and realizing that—in your opinion—the client didn't use your best work? The answer is simple.

Yes, you have power. You are important. You are the talent. You have a lot of knowledge. You are creative. You are unique because no one does it quite like you. But remember, you were *hired* for a job. You work for hire. The client thought the take he chose was the best one—so you have to let it go. That *was* the best take.

Your opinion doesn't matter or count—unless the client asks for it.

Actually, I'm happiest when they don't ask for my opinion—because it means the clients know what they want. My job is to give them what they want, and let them give the final answer as to whether or not it's good. So, it all goes back to "If they like it, leave." When the client decides you're done, you're done.

Contributing Ideas

Sometimes a director or client will indicate that he or she wants you to contribute your ideas and comments. It feels like a loose and collaborative project. However, if the session is tense, if there is a tight deadline, or if the director is telling you exactly what to do on every take, chances are you should save your input for another day.

Loose and collaborative clients like creative people. That's why they have you there. They like improvisation. They expect you to be improvisational, they expect you to be creative, and they expect you to be knowledgeable about what you've been hired for.

Working within the framework of a team concept makes the collaborative process much easier. You don't have to step out of your area unless you are asked to.

Giving One Hundred and Ten Percent

Some voice-over actors worry about being exploited if they offer to do extra work, like suggesting new copy or giving ideas for different ways to play characters. It's true, some people in this business will take everything you offer without so much as a thank you.

I don't offer anything I don't want to provide. If I have an idea and I'm willing to do the work that goes with it, I'll offer the idea. The other aspect of my positive approach is that I keep in mind the final product is me. In other words, the better the session goes, the better I sound in the final product.

When you're in a situation where extra work is called for, remember that it's you who is shining, it's you who is putting good karma in the universe, and it's you who is going to get another job from that employer because they know your work ethic. They know the extent of your contributions and how much you enhanced the final product. Or, perhaps, some other employer will hear your voice on that spot, and hire you because they thought it was great.

Make the extra work okay by remembering the final product is you.

Your positive attitude is: "They've asked me to do a little more than I'm being paid for, but I'm interested in the overall outcome of the project. I will make this contribution. I can do this out of the goodness of my heart and because of the positive attitude I have. In the end, I'm going to benefit from these gifts that I've laid on them. People are going to give gifts to me."

When you give, it comes back.

If you shine in a session by going above and beyond what's expected of you, you make yourself more desirable in the future. The word's out—you're a team player!

THE EXTRA EFFORT GETS THE JOB

I received a call from my agent one day requesting a CD of my promo demo reel. He also asked me to send a lot of extra copies to the agency, because they were out of them. It wasn't normal for him to personally call me with a demo request, so I asked him what he needed it for. He informed me that one of the major networks was considering hiring me to do promos for one of their hit summer programs.

Now, one would think that since I had worked for this network many times over the years, the people there would be familiar with my work. And, if the situation was so urgent, couldn't I just send them an audio file over the Internet in the form of an MP3 or WAVE file? Plus, I have my own website, so couldn't they go there and listen to my work?

This request is ridiculous, I thought. *I'm not traveling all the way over to Beverly Hills to drop off a CD that my agent can deliver to the network.*

Well, thank God that bit of nonsensical thinking was brief. I jumped in my car and took the last five CDs I had to my agent. He had a messenger take the demo to the network—and I got the job.

It turns out the producer who hired me had been a fan of my work for years. He was trying to convince his bosses to use me. They did, in fact, visit my website to listen to my promo work. They also listened to past work that I had done for their network. But, there was one person there who still believed in the formal CD demo. Not only did he want to physically hold the demo in his hand, he wanted to add it to the network's files for future reference.

There was a great lesson learned here. Technology has made us take the shortest route—the easy way out of everything. Need me to record a session? Hey, dial me up on my ISDN line. Want to hear a sample of my work? Give me your e-mail address, I'll send you an MP3. You need it quicker than that? Go to my website.

I'm not saying these methods are wrong, but don't neglect the CD demo. It is still an industry standard that is utilized, expected, and accepted in many powerful circles today.

The personal touch is still required in some circles, so provide it whenever it is requested. Go to your auditions. Go to your sessions. Don't always "phone it in." You have to be willing to go that extra mile if you want to get the job.

---

*If you shine in a session by going
above and beyond what's expected of
you, you make yourself more desirable
in the future.*

Building Allies

It's important to form a team of allies when you are trying to be successful in the entertainment industry. Allies are good, positive individuals who have your best interest at heart. They make you feel good.

They tell you when they think something could be detrimental to your character, career, or overall well-being.

Allies are your own personal army. The camaraderie of people from all walks of life—not just your profession, but the banker, teacher, doctor, or plumber whom you befriend—can provide inspiring and comforting words when you need a pick-me-up.

Employers who are more than satisfied with your work and hire you over and over again are part of your army too. You can use them as references when you recruit new candidates to employ you, admire you, and become soldiers in your army. Before you know it, you will amass a surprising number of believers who will knock down walls for you.

No matter how strongly you may think you are alone, there is nothing more powerful than having numbers of folks fighting for your cause.

Positive Networking

Some of you are not the most social people in the world. You tend to shy away from people, you don't attend industry functions, and you pride yourselves on being reclusive individuals. This is okay in some occupations, but it's a big mistake in the voice-over community. Bonding with your peers is of paramount importance if you want to hear about the latest projects that need talent like yours.

When you network in a positive way, you will encourage others to tell you about hot job opportunities. If you share and share alike, you will be constantly blessed with tips about trends, events, and other matters crucial to the advancement of your career. Choose to share your working life with like-minded friends. Toss around strategies and marketing ideas with the understanding that you can help each other by brainstorming creative methods together.

Don't network with just anybody. Cultivate trustworthy relationships, which are hard to come by, and even harder to find, if you don't go out and seek them.

Positive networking is healthy.

The Positive Pre-Beat

When you take a step, make sure the step that follows the first one doesn't take you into a brick wall or into the deep end of a swimming pool. When you read copy, or speak to a director or another actor, there's a pause before the cause.

In other words, a moment of positive thought precedes your positive action. A positive action precedes the main action. That positive pre-action is called the pre-beat. You should use pre-beats in everything you do. If you don't, you will constantly insult people because you haven't taken the time to censor your remarks and comments.

Basically a pre-beat is a commonsense reflex; but you need to take this natural reflex out of your subconscious and move it to your conscious state—where you can control an event and make it have a positive outcome.

Take time to think before you act. You can't un-ring a bell. It's a matter of milliseconds that you have to do the right thing, but you can gain control by bringing the pre-beat concept into your everyday existence and letting it become a conscious, positive tool in your life.

"In the end, we will remember not the words of our enemies, but the silence of our friends."

—MARTIN LUTHER KING JR.

Let a Positive Attitude Become Your Brand

People talk about branding in business all the time—developing a brand that customers buy because they are familiar with it. Casting directors audition you and producers cast you repeatedly because they are happy and familiar with your brand. Not just how you sound, but your attitude.

Let me give you a scenario. Voice actress "A" is very talented; but she has a negative attitude. She's arrogant and abrasive. Generally, she is not a pleasant person to be around. Voice actress "B" is equally talented and has a positive attitude. She is confident yet humble and generally makes everyone around her feel good about her and themselves. Given their equal talent, hiring one over the other comes down to preference.

The bottom line is producers and casting directors like to do business with actors they feel better about. This is called preference, and preference creates work for performers with positive attitudes.

POSITIVE THOUGHTS

Maintain a positive attitude
at all times, and conquer
the voice-over world!

Positive Feedback

How many people do you know who want to hear the truth about what you think of sensitive issues in their lives, like their looks, intelligence, or career? I would venture to say you don't know many people like this. As much as we think we can handle the truth about what others think about us, we can't.

My mother often said to me, "If you can't say something nice about a person, don't say anything at all." I paid attention to this advice and, although I haven't been perfect, I have certainly tried to live my life that way.

Now, don't get me wrong. I have discussed the value of being honest with yourself throughout this book, but being true to yourself and using truthful words of negativity with someone else are two completely different actions.

You want to avoid being rude; so, if you must critique, do it in a way that is instructive, constructive, and informative. It is far better to err on the side of being too positive with your fellow actors.

If you are a person that thrives on feedback, make sure you can handle the negative feedback because not everyone is as tactful as you would like them to be.

Reject all feedback from people you don't respect. Their words—positive or negative—are just words to you, because you don't respect them. Maybe they are not experts in your field or perhaps they generally don't have your best interest at heart.

MAXIMIZE YOUR SUCCESS

Pump up the volume and get more success by working ten times harder. Keep growing.

Surround yourself with positive people and you will always receive constructive positive feedback.

"If indeed you must be candid, be candid beautifully."

—Kahlil Gibran

Promote Your Positive Image

You must conduct yourself in an upbeat manner at all times if you want to promote a positive and professional image. If you are generally kind to your competition, directors, engineers, writers, and agents, you will make the workplace a positive environment for you and everyone around you.

Here are some themes to incorporate into your workday:

○ Don't engage in gossip or conspire against others.

○ Welcome constructive criticism from the director.

○ Exude confidence, not arrogance.

○ Always strive to do quality work.

○ Be on time.

Pay It Forward

In 2000, I saw the movie *Pay It Forward*, starring Kevin Spacey, Helen Hunt, and Haley Joel Osment. The premise of the movie was to pass along a good deed to someone and then that person would in turn pass a good deed on to someone else. I left the theater inspired to do the same thing: pass good deeds onto others.

I often meet people, young and old, who express a keen interest in getting into the voice-over industry. I decided to help them get into the business by sharing my knowledge and experience.

> You will find that the mere resolve not to be useless, and the honest desire to help other people, will, in the quickest and delicatest ways, improve yourself.
>
> —JOHN RUSKIN

I found myself giving advice to total strangers—in restaurants, stores, or in line at the bank. These people would marvel at my occupation when it came up in casual conversation.

It feels good to share my blessings. There is no benefit in not doing so. And I find that the more I give, the more I get.

When you serve others, you almost always reap the rewards. In many ways, it is wrong to hoard your good fortune because, if you really think about it, someone directed you to your winnings. Someone intentionally or unwittingly paid it forward to you. And

so, it is your spiritual and positive duty to help someone less fortunate than you.

Help another actor find an agent or a good acting
class if you know of one. Perhaps you know a producer
who does great voice-over demos; let people know
about that person. When you devote your energy to
being a good citizen, you are promoting a positive way
of life.

CHAPTER 8

Useful
Empowerment Exercises

I HOPE YOU REALIZE THAT HAVING A POSITIVE ATTITUDE is a blessing, not a burden. Sure, it may seem like hard work—to look at every situation in a positive way—but think about what you receive. Taking the high road wins you the respect of your coworkers and provides for steady employment in the voice-over business. Now—those are two things all of us can be positive about!

In this chapter, I provide simple exercises you can do to keep the positive energy flowing day after day.

Affirmations

What is an affirmation? An affirmation is a declaration or statement about a positive action or actions that a person wants to have occur in his or her life. It is a powerful tool for making your dreams manifest.

People have used affirmations for hundreds of years to make their desires and dreams reality. For a long time, it has been believed that the subconscious mind cannot differentiate between actual reality and wishes or suggestions. Consequently, your mind processes affirmations of your dreams as being real. Eventually, those affirmations come true.

In order to maximize the innate power of affirmations, you should repeat the following words with feeling. You must be emotional about these desires and give boundless energy to saying these words daily, weekly, or monthly.

Let there be no physical, emotional, or mental tension while you say your affirmations. The stronger your desire and concentration, the more faith you will have in what you are seeking.

Find the level of repetition that works for you. You can add, delete, and modify these affirmations to suit your needs.

Repeat these words, and make them come true:

- I will do things today to make work for tomorrow.
- A national television commercial campaign is in my immediate future.
- My career will bring me peace, money, and inner strength forever.
- Today I will get a job I never auditioned for.
- A former employer will recommend me for a major job.

○ I will always be the best that I can be in auditions.

○ Today I will get a voice-over job that will pay six figures.

○ Today I will get a regular role on an animation series.

The I-See-Myself Exercise

Take a look at the affirmations listed below and choose the one(s) that apply to you. Repeat each line twice. Start each sentence with these three words, "I see myself . . . "

○ going into public speaking

○ improving my booking ratio

○ rising above my limitations

○ helping others achieve their goals

○ going beyond my wildest dreams

○ captivating audiences with my voice

○ at the bank, cashing large residual checks

○ happy and content with my career choices

○ making my future bigger than my past

○ releasing the brakes and accelerating my career

By stating these affirmations, you consciously embrace the ideas and constructively direct your voice-over thoughts and goals. Some people choose to close their eyes and meditate. They see their goals through the practice of visualization.

These positive words will make you better and stronger in your auditions and your work. Every aspect of your career will be affected by this exercise. Hopefully, all of your dreams and goals will manifest quickly.

There have been times in my life when going through this ritual gave me everything I needed to face the day. Many times, because I put these affirmations into the universe, they came true immediately.

Interactive Voice-Over Affirmations

Close your eyes and think nothing but positive thoughts. Draw an imaginary circle in the air with your index finger. Then, with your eyes still closed, put your finger on one of the affirmations in the following boxes. Whichever one you choose, make that the way you will feel your entire day.

HAPPY	**HAPPIER**
BLESSED	**MORE BLESSED**
CONFIDENT	**MORE CONFIDENT**

Interactive Voice-Over Exercise

Close your eyes. Draw an imaginary circle in the air with your index finger and say the words: "Today I will book a . . ." Then, put your finger on one of the boxes below, open your eyes, and finish the sentence with the words in the box. Your desire to achieve this goal is now in the universe. You've said it, now go and claim it.

A NATIONAL COMMERCIAL	**AN ANIMATED SERIES**
A BOOK ON TAPE	**A TELEVISION PROMO**
A VIDEO GAME	**A VOICE PROMPT**

The Mirror Exercise

From time to time, we have all talked to ourselves. Well, let's take this one step further.

Look in the mirror and talk to your image. Ask yourself this question: "Do I like me?" The answer to that question is important. If you don't like yourself, you are in a heap of trouble. We're not comfortable with people and things we don't like. We try to avoid them at all costs.

You have to learn to not only like yourself, but also to love yourself. Come to grips with what it is you don't like about yourself, and work on fixing those things immediately. Your self-image is what gives you the confidence that makes others enjoy your company. Employers will notice your self-confidence and react to it in a positive way. Your auditions will be stronger and your booking ratio will be much higher.

Affirm your wants and desires, and discuss your strategies to make them into reality. The man or woman in the mirror can't lie or deceive you, because you can judge him or her by looking into his or her eyes.

The eyes never lie. You will be able to look in the mirror and see the truth about how badly you really want what you affirmed. When you watch yourself state your desires, you can tell if you're really willing to put in the work to get them.

When you finish working in the mirror, you will have trimmed the fat—it will be clear what is real and achievable, and what is just a passing fancy.

The mirror exercise helps you be true to yourself.

Which Hat Will I Wear Today?

Have you ever dedicated an entire day to attaining a single goal? Doing this can lead to powerful results. For instance, put on your actor hat and read scripts all day. Or put on your agent hat and search the Internet all day for agencies that could represent you.

This exercise helps you focus on specific goals. You put on a designated hat to represent each goal that you are trying to achieve. Give it a go!

LIVE YOUR DREAMS

If you dream of living your life as a voice-over artist, then do it!

Pick a Positive Behavior Exercise

Below is a list of 42 actions. Place a check next to the ones you think you would really do—and then go out and do them.

- ❐ Eat right
- ❐ Practice new dialects
- ❐ Be kind to others
- ❐ Get proper rest
- ❐ Pray
- ❐ Agree to grow
- ❐ Listen
- ❐ Exercise
- ❐ Laugh
- ❐ Prioritize
- ❐ Show passion
- ❐ Erase doubt
- ❐ Walk in the light of faith
- ❐ Self-motivate
- ❐ Research
- ❐ Seek knowledge
- ❐ Smell the roses
- ❐ Meditate
- ❐ Strategize
- ❐ Read self-help books
- ❐ Create employment in your field
- ❐ Be polite
- ❐ Focus
- ❐ Treat yourself
- ❐ Call employers
- ❐ Take a vacation
- ❐ Go to a movie
- ❐ Be truthful
- ❐ Be contrite
- ❐ Dream
- ❐ Be fearless
- ❐ Care
- ❐ Ask questions
- ❐ Network
- ❐ Cry tears of joy
- ❐ Give thanks
- ❐ Apologize
- ❐ Party
- ❐ Enjoy every day
- ❐ Compete
- ❐ Excel
- ❐ Donate your time and money

Random Questions

This exercise is designed to give you an idea of who you are as a voice-over artist—your likes, dislikes, and competency in various areas of the business.

Fill in the circle to indicate your answer.

1. How much time in a week do you spend looking for voice-over work?

    ○ 10%
    ○ 20%
    ○ 50%
    ○ 100%

2. Which statement best describes your level of positive thinking?

    ○ I'm a very positive thinker
    ○ I'm a moderately positive thinker
    ○ I'm not a positive thinker

3. Which statement best describes your level of optimism?

    ○ I'm very optimistic
    ○ I'm moderately optimistic
    ○ I'm not an optimist

4. Rate your competence in the following activities (1 being most competent and 4 being not competent).

	1	2	3	4
Auditions	○	○	○	○
Reading Copy	○	○	○	○
Interpreting Copy	○	○	○	○
Group Copy	○	○	○	○
Dialects	○	○	○	○

5. Rank the following categories that you want to work in (1 being most desirable and 3 being the least).

	1	2	3
Commercial	O	O	O
Animation	O	O	O
Books on Tape	O	O	O

6. If you could choose your voice-over destiny, which would you choose (1 being most important and 4 being the least)?

	1	2	3	4
To be rich	O	O	O	O
To work steady	O	O	O	O
To quit the business	O	O	O	O
To be happy	O	O	O	O
To be content	O	O	O	O

7. How many times during the week do you say something positive to another voice-over talent?

0	1-2	3-5	6+
O	O	O	O

8. Which of these items have you purchased for your voice?
    - O Books
    - O Throat lozenges
    - O Vocal coaching
    - O Recording equipment
    - O Insurance policy

9.   How much money are you willing to spend on your voice-over career over a period of one year?

○ Less than $500
○ $500 to $1,000
○ $1,000 to $5,000
○ $10,000+

10.   Demographic Questions

Age _____
Gender _____
Region _____
Years of experience _____
Annual salary _____

Give Yourself a High Five

Ever since I was two years old, I've been slapping my hand upside another person's hand in the name of a positive physical action affectionately called a "high five." I think my dad and uncles were the first to press my palms—but it wasn't long before my mother and aunts were saying to me, "Give me five, Rodney."

When I got older, my friends and I would say things like: "give me a pound," or "give me some skin." And when my reaction was slow, I was told, "Don't leave me hanging."

No matter what is said during the interaction, people know what it means to "Give me a high five." Now it's time to high-five yourself.

Write down five positive things that you did each day for five days, and give yourself a congratulatory high five by slapping your palms together after each one.

DAY ONE

1. _____

2. _____

3. _____

4. _____

5. _____

DAY TWO

1. _____

2. _____

3. _____

4. _____

5. _____

DAY THREE

1. _____

2. _____

3. _____

4. _____

5. _____

DAY FOUR

1. _____
2. _____
3. _____
4. _____
5. _____

DAY FIVE

1. _____
2. _____
3. _____
4. _____
5. _____

Ten Tips to Ignite Your Voice-Over Career

1. Be creative
2. Think about the big picture
3. Keep an open mind
4. Take time to make time
5. Give yourself the opportunity to be your best
6. Be true to yourself and others
7. Define your intentions
8. Stay positive
9. Keep it simple
10. Never underestimate your power

What are You Joyful About?

Write a list of the things that bring you joy—both at home and on the job. You might be surprised by how much joy is already in your abundant life. To get an idea of how to do this exercise, here's my list:

I'm joyful about:

Being in the voice-over industry

Doing something I love and would do for free

Being healthy both physically and mentally

Teaching what I have learned to others

Waking up every morning

Being strong in my faith

Being employed in the industry

Being willing and able to grow

Being able to love myself

Being able to love and help others

The Five W's Exercise

Here is an exercise you should do every day to get into a positive frame of mind. Go through these questions and answers each morning before you start your day, filling in your own specific information if you want to.

WHO (Who are you?)   Your Name

WHAT (What are you?)   A working voice-
                                       over artist

WHEN (When are you a voice-over artist?)   Right now

WHERE (Where are you a voice-over artist?) In studios all
                                        over the country

WHY (Why are you a voice-over artist?)   Because I love it

When you put it all together, it should sound like this: "Who am I? I'm Rodney. What am I? I'm a working voice-over artist. When? Right now. Where? In studios all over the country. Why? Because I love it."

Go over this list until you are ready to start your day.

CHAPTER 9

All About You

WE HAVE DISCUSSED HOW YOUR POSITIVE attitude benefits others—now we are going to focus on you. This is your voice-over career, so enjoy it! Don't overwork it.

It is not necessary to memorize voice-over copy. The script is always there, so you are never at a loss for words. Sessions get complicated when you make them complicated. You overwork it. You over think it. You try too hard to enunciate, or to be clever and funny.

Remember, sometimes less is more. Effortlessness can be powerful. Just letting it happen is sometimes the best way to go.

No Is Not a Bad Word

Saying no can be a very positive response when it

benefits you and the party you are rejecting. If there is a business event you don't want to attend or a voice-over job you don't want to do, you should respectfully decline.

You must have the ability to say no. If there is an opportunity for diplomacy, be diplomatic, but there will be times when you have to emphatically disappoint someone whom you hold in high regard. When you stand your ground, you avoid a bigger confrontation that could occur if you do something you really don't want to do—which could be more detrimental in the long run than your immediate no.

When you say no, you will probably feel a sense of relief. The person you said no to hurts a little longer than you—but they get over it, too. Develop the ability to JUST SAY NO! It's a positive and admirable quality.

Physical Fitness

For those of us who are committed to voice-overs as our only means of employment, our physical fitness is at risk. Since we work in a segment of the entertainment community that doesn't make the way we look a criterion for hiring, we sometimes have a tendency to not push away from the table in general, let alone on those festive and food-abundant holidays.

It's easy to fall into the trap of eating what you want and not exercising, which is an unhealthy habit. If you are not healthy, ultimately, you won't be happy. Even if you have been getting away with an improper diet and a sedentary lifestyle, you are only cheating yourself because you could be a hundred times better if you were in top-notch physical condition.

You need stamina to read long passages of copy. You need energy to go after all of the wonderful jobs that are out there waiting for you to claim. It's hard to last long in any career if you don't have a positive hold on your physical well-being.

It is a negative proposition when you ignore the temple that houses the most precious God-given gift you own, your voice. Starting today, take control of your diet and overall physical fitness. Turn your negative eating and exercising habits into positive, healthy habits that will ensure a long and prosperous voice-over career.

How can you fit healthy, nutritious habits into your fast-paced lifestyle and budget? Before you go to the grocery store, make a list of healthy foods to buy, including fresh fruit and vegetables. Read the labels on packaged goods, so that you make wise choices. If your budget is tight, look around for the best prices. You can do it. I know you can.

Money Matters

Set financial goals that include how much money you plan to earn and how much you plan to spend. Basically, the sky is the limit on how much money you can make in this business—so think big!

Be wise with your purchases. Prioritize. Following are examples of positive and negative purchases relative to your voice-over career.

Positive Buys

Inexpensive Recording Equipment

Two great sources when equipping your home studio are:

In *The Voice Actor's Guide to Home Recording*, Jeffrey P. Fisher and Harlan Hogan write about reasonably priced home studio equipment.

James Alburger lists excellent information about inexpensive gear on his website at www.jamesalburger.com.

Industry Magazines

These publications give you information on the whereabouts of casting directors, agents, producers, coaches, and all things related to the advancement of your career.

Negative Buys

Buying Representation

Don't pay someone upfront money to represent you. You don't need to purchase a "like" of your talent. If an agent or manager believes in you, he or she should love to do so—without enticement. They get paid after they get you a job.

Expensive Coaching

Generally, you should pay the market rate for voice-over coaching. If someone is way beyond the range of others in their category, you should probably not hire them.

On the other hand, if your budget can handle it and after comparisons and research you are convinced this coach is worth the extra dollars, go for it.

KNOWLEDGE IS POWER

The more you know, the better you will be. You're only nervous when you don't know what you're doing.

Learning With Your Ears

Listening is critical to a voice-over career because when you listen to relatives, neighbors, and other people with interesting voices, you can learn how they talk and you try to mimic them.

For instance, one member of my family's voice has always caught my ear. I have used his voice many times because I think of him while I perform different characters. One of my most popular characters is the jazzman in the Zatarain's commercials. This relative speaks with a particular dialect; he says things like: "Well, I'm just gonna be frank witcha" (I'm going to be frank with you) and "Whatchu say?" (What did you say?). Out of him was born the Zatarain's jazzman.

Exciting voices that catch your interest are references you can use for characters throughout your career. As a voice-over artist, you learn when you listen.

In the voice-over world, your mind is like a tape recorder or a hard disc. You file away voices, events, and other things in your life to use later.

A voice-over artist needs a good memory, just like actors do. You should always be recording and absorbing sounds to use in your work.

You don't always need a character description to go into a certain voice or style. Although it would be easier to follow a written description found at the top of the script, sometimes the words within the copy lend themselves to a particular kind of performance.

I recently did voice work on a short film. It's ten

minutes long, it's entertaining, and I play the narrator. Based on the content and style of the copy, I read the narration in a certain voice. I wasn't given a character description—I was narrating.

But, the director had a vision and knew how he wanted the voice to sound. Based on his direction and the words in the script, I came up with a particular voice. I was able to do it by using one of the many voices stored in my mental tape recorder.

"Memory feeds imagination."
—AMY TAN

Listen Before You Talk

Obviously, when you work on dialogue copy with other actors, you need to listen intently to the actors who speak before and after you. Your reactions and responses will be better if you do so. Your interpretation of the words you speak will be more in line with what the copywriter intended for you to convey.

Find Your Natural Voice

Do you know who you are vocally? The commercial industry no longer wants performers who think they can do a lot of voices. That's a great attribute, especially for animation, but I'm talking about your specific sound. The industry wants people with signature sounds; so you have to find the unique sound that is you.

The current trend in the commercial community is "real-sounding everyday people." Producers and casting directors want to hear the natural you. If this is a problem for you, you need to find out what is stopping you from being who you really are. When you're in a session, do you get direction to "be yourself" behind the mic, even though you can't seem to figure out who that self really is?

That is the goal you have to reach—the ability to know what your natural voice is and to dial it up on request.

Some people think the "announcer" sound is completely passé, but I disagree. Don't abandon your announcer chops if you have them. Even though most of the performers in commercials today need to sound natural, many spots still have a traditional announcer reading the announcer copy.

Your Attitude Is Everything

Your attitude will determine how you feel mentally and physically all day long. The moment you wake up, you can choose to be happy or sad. You have the ability to set the tone the minute your feet touch the floor. Extenuating circumstances beyond your control, such as the death of a loved one or a sudden physical ailment that overcomes you, are understandable. But there is nothing else that should stand in the way of you deciding to have a pleasant day filled with reasons to smile.

Once you decide to be happy, busy yourself with things to do. Don't be afraid to multitask. It's okay if all your tasks are related to furthering your voice-over career, and it's okay if they don't relate.

Take your destiny into your own hands. Don't depend on others to help you pay your monthly bills. Become the CEO (Chief Executive Officer) of your career.

When I took the steps to make my career a positive reality, I was willing to take chances and go for it. One day I just looked in the mirror and said, "I'm going to take the credit or the blame."

You have to have goals to aim for. If you aim for nothing, you'll hit that target every time. Don't be jealous when others around you are experiencing success. Your ship is coming in soon. It's right around the corner if you walk in the light of a positive attitude.

"Be not afraid of growing slowly, be afraid of standing still."

—CHINESE PROVERB

How to Cope With Stress

If anybody ever tells you that they don't experience stress in this business, they are probably not being honest with you or themselves. All voice-over actors suffer from stress from time to time—and it isn't always stress that comes from not having work. You can be stressed in fruitful times, when you're booking ninety percent of what you audition for.

It doesn't matter if your stress is warranted or not in the eyes of others. The most important thing is how you deal with it.

My recommendation is to think about what is really important in your life. For most people, that would be their health and the health of their loved ones. As much as you love your work, it should not be the most important thing in your life.

Focus on your blessings. Put those things up against any commercial you didn't book, and I guarantee you will conquer your stress. The bigger disappointments hurt a little longer, but they too will dissipate in time.

The combination of acknowledging your blessings and the passage of time is a powerful antidote to whatever ails you emotionally.

Stress is a killer. We are part of a business that specializes in the art of rejection. If you don't learn how to deal with rejection, you will not survive. It's hard to accept that sometimes you are not perfect, but you must. Remember, being a perfectionist means being afraid to show any flaws. That is an impossible task.

Set a Personal Bar

Sports are competitive. Beauty pageants and high school debate teams are, too. We learn early in life that competition is a major part of life. The people who win these contests are the ones who recognize who their competition really is. Your competition is you.

The quicker you grasp this concept, the quicker you will start winning. It's okay to admire others. It's okay to have mentors and to be impressed by other people. It is not, however, okay to let them set your standards of achievement.

Everyone is different and marches to his or her own drum. For some reason, we often choose to ignore our individuality and morph into a copy of another person's persona.

No one can be you better than you. Cultivate your own style. Find your signature voice. Set your own bar, and rise to it. Be the best that you can be. Surpass your latest accomplishments with even loftier goals and achievements.

Compete with yourself. Push yourself. When you attain the position you decided to go after and you are satisfied with your accomplishment, that's good enough.

"Action is the foundational key
to all success."

—TONY ROBBINS

You Have to Go for It

Write this down on a sheet of paper: "Today I will take the proper path to *step up to the mic* and pursue a prosperous and lucrative career in voice-overs."

The proper path is the road to success. That road is paved in voice-over gold. It's shiny, it's rewarding, and it is possible. If you believe it is possible, it will happen. Claim it!

There is one easy way out of everything. You know what that is? To quit. If you can't stand the heat, all you have to do is get out of the kitchen. But how rewarding would that be?

Take action! Give yourself a chance to compete. You can do it, but you won't know until you give it your level best.

NEVER GIVE UP

Be fearless in your climb to succeed. In order to stay in the game you must play the game. Don't quit!

Get in Touch With the Winner in You

All of us have had victories in our lives. Even the smallest victory counts as a positive moment. Think about what that positive moment felt like, and try to rekindle the feeling. Learn how to recall that victory when you are faced with defeat. If you can do this, you can force yourself to eliminate negative energy.

The ability to get in touch with the winner in you is necessary for dealing with the constant rejection you will face in the voice-over industry. It's comforting to know that if you can think about the good times in your past, you can ease your present pain more quickly.

When I didn't get the commercial I auditioned for last week—even though it was down to just me and another actor—I eased the pain by conjuring up the good feelings I had when I was the winner of a major national commercial campaign two years ago.

Believe me, it works.

Your Voice-Over Frame of Mind

When you audition and when you work on the job, you must be in a certain frame of mind to function and create a euphoric, positive atmosphere. This frame of mind is so powerful it becomes contagious. Everyone in the vicinity will feel your energy and adopt your glow. Consequently, they will always want you around because you make them feel good. You make them glow.

Don't get the wrong idea—I don't operate in an unrealistic realm. I am a realist. But I'm not a pessimist. I am a dreamer who strives to make my dreams and goals come true—and that kind of positive energy excites everyone I meet. If you adopt an uplifting attitude, you will also raise the spirits of everyone you meet.

Be Confident In Your Uniqueness

Knowing who you are—and how unique you are—helps you keep a positive attitude, because you know that no one can "do" you better than you.

Clients hire you because they like what you have to offer, so you're already ahead of the game once you discover your signature voice. That's an important thing to remember. Believe it or not, you're in power—because your talent is unique. Not everybody can do what you can do.

This alone should give you confidence. Just think about it. Your voice is the voice that goes out to thousands or even millions of people to entice them to buy a product or believe in a character. You are powerful. Your confidence comes from knowing that you have an instrument that is unique to you. Clients believe your instrument will help them sell their products.

"Insist on yourself, never imitate. . . .
Every great man is unique."
—RALPH WALDO EMERSON

If It's for Real, You Will Stay the Course

About twenty years ago I saw the late Richard Pryor perform his stand-up comedy routine at the

THERE IS ONLY ONE U

Maintain your uniqueness. Find your signature voice and remember, no one can do "you" better than you.

Comedy Store on Sunset Boulevard in Hollywood. The next day, I set out to be a stand-up comedian. I toiled away for a few months, and actually took the stage on amateur night at the Comedy Store. I failed miserably. It wasn't for real and I wasn't for real, so I moved on.

I also watched the great boxer Sugar Ray Leonard defeat Thomas Hearns for the World Welterweight Title, and thought I could become a boxer. It wasn't for real and I wasn't for real. The dream faded.

My love for voice-over work and my interest in making a living with my voice would not let me go. I couldn't shake my desire to be successful. I was passionate about it. I worked hard to succeed and,

PASSION

Now the time is here
Now it's pretty clear
That you don't really know what you want to do

You could style hair
Work at the shoe repair
But to your heart would you really be true?

You want to feel the tingle
Brag when you intermingle
About this profession that makes you feel brand-new

To anyone who'll listen
You'll tell them what they're missin
And that if you can do it, they can do it too

There'll be no way to hide it
You'll wear it like you pride it
A smile so big, through doors you can't get through

When you land on the planet satisfied
A sense of calm you'll feel inside
Because you finally found something you love to do

—*Rodney Saulsberry*

eventually, I was very successful. It was for real and I stayed the course.

If you embark on a career in the voice-over industry and it's for real, you will stay the course.

Passion is the key.

"In order that people may be happy in their work, these three things are needed. They must be fit for it. They must not do too much of it. And they must have a sense of success in it."

— JOHN RUSKIN

Work Is Its Own Reward

Every day you work is wonderful; remember that each time you arrive at an assignment. The joy is in having the job. You should realize you are in a business in which most people don't work regularly. So, if you are working, it's naturally a positive situation.

The way to hold on to that positive energy is to keep thinking about the job you're doing or the job you're about to do. That's the simple answer—it doesn't get any deeper than that.

SECTION III

INSPIRATIONAL & MOTIVATIONAL CONTRIBUTIONS

CHAPTER 10

Let's Review

O KAY, NOW IT'S TIME TO FLIP ON THE SWITCH and turn on the lights. Let's find out how well you have retained the information presented to you so far in this book.

Hopefully you have gathered enough positive reinforcement principles to form an *action plan* to put your positive attitude into play in the workplace.

There will no longer be any *procrastination* in your life, however, you must think in terms of looking *long-term* as you travel on your journey to being the best you can be. Along the way, you must be willing to *shift gears* if you have to, to get there. Your eyes must always *be on the prize*—but your peripheral vision had better be sharp or you just might miss a *golden opportunity* that is right *under your nose*.

Be your own boss or stay trapped in the cubicle of someone else's vision of who you are. Beware of those who ask you: "Are you ready to move to a *new con-*

Stick to your objectives
Take your time
Renew your faith
Initiate new challenges
Victory is your goal
Excellence will be your reward

cept?" If it's a concept that promotes negativity, your answer should always be an unequivocal no.

No concept beats the power of positive thinking. *Focus on the positives* in your life and you will be able to strike a balance between work, family, and leisure. When you strike this balance, you gain control.

Control means working in the voice-over business

that you love and actually having the time to do it. Through thick and thin it is always important to *know thy worth*. Only then will you have the power to demand what you are worth.

When you carry yourself erect with extreme self-confidence, you will demand respect and high compensation for your efforts from others. Control the present and control your future. You are the captain of your ship. *Life is what you make it.*

Treasure your mere existence by loving thy self and taking care of your mind, body, and soul. *You have to be your number one fan!*

Chapter 11

Words of Wisdom From the Pros

N OW THAT YOU KNOW HOW I FEEL ABOUT the power of a positive attitude, I want you to learn from some other consummate professionals who were kind enough to contribute their thoughts on the subject. I asked each of them to respond to this question: *How has a positive attitude helped you in your career?* In alphabetical order, here's what they had to say.

DISCLAIMER

Contributors to this chapter are not by way of their contributions endorsing the other content in this book. Their contributions, as well as the author's, are born solely of their own opinions and beliefs.

"Having a positive attitude is, in my opinion, one of THE most important things in achieving success. In fact, if you take everything seriously, serious everything will be— I promise. I make a point of having fun in my life, and in my career, and you should, too. Young or old, having a little insouciance (being carefree) can make all the difference in meeting the right people at the right time and getting the right job for you. Love what you do, have fun with it, and see if you don't feel just a little bit happier about yourself, and you might even find achieving your goals becomes easier, especially in voice-acting, where the competition is fierce and the voices are many.

"This is one of my 'having a good life' policies: *If I'm not having fun, something is wrong.* As a professional, of course, my immediate goal when I go to work is to 'get the job done as best I can.' And you should too, but you deal with a lot of personalities in this business, and being known as a curmudgeon does not help you. I don't invite everyone from work to my home, but the truth is I have to be able to get along with EVERYONE I work with and so I adopt a positive attitude. It is sound advice that someone near and dear to me told me years ago, and when I apply it, it works! Now, go ahead and give it a try—right now! Decide to be more positive in your life and in your career . . . wax enthusiastic if you have to, but keep "putting it there" until you feel it in your heart. You will do yourself a world of good—and all those you come in contact with!"

~ NANCY CARTWRIGHT, best known as the voice of
Bart Simpson from the animated television
series, *The Simpsons,* and author of the
bestseller *My Life as a Ten-Year-Old Boy.*

"I have to say one word covers it all: TENACITY. Don't ever give up! Absolutely, positively TAKE NO PRIS-ONERS in your personal quest to win the battles you ultimately will face over the span of your career. Mind you, I am not advocating that you can't display compassion, courtesy and respect to those you meet along the way. But there will be forces out there who, for one reason or another, want you to fail. That goes for friends, family, ex-wives, ex-husbands, etc.—and sometimes surprisingly, your agent!! I take pride in the fact that I am part of, although comparatively small, an elite group of performers who know the craft of voice-over acting.

"So, learn your craft well. Do your homework at home, NOT IN THE RECORDING STUDIO. Study not only self-help texts such as this; but take a V.O. class, study the trends in commercial advertising and trailer and TV production. Learn your craft so you know craft!! Most of all, develop your own indelible style and signature. Lord knows, we've got enough "voice replicants" and "voice whisperers" out there! Even in this age, uniqueness still means something special. YOUR uniqueness is your gift. YOUR gift is your crown. Put it on and wear it proudly! So, take two, and I'll see you at the movies!"

~ AL CHALK, best known as the trailer voice
for the *Scary Movie* franchise and the
new animated movie *Flushed Away*.

"A positive attitude has helped my career in every which way. First of all, it helped stop me from feeling like a victim or feeling that life was fair. I never thought that I ever lost a job, but it was an opportunity to step up to the plate. So, there was never any looking back. A positive attitude helped me also in the fact that any kind of achievement I would enjoy was an opportunity to help other people. Quite frankly, that's what has always given me more joy than anything else. And it all started by not feeling like a victim.

"So, that's it. I've been very, very fortunate. My positive attitude is the way I look at the world. It's my inner philosophy. Expect the ball to take a bad hop, and when it doesn't, take advantage of it by reaching out and helping others."

~ HECTOR ELIZONDO, best known as Dr. Phillip Watters from the critically acclaimed television series *Chicago Hope*. His voice-over credits include the voice of Chevron.

"One needs a positive attitude to survive in this business. It is not a fair business, but then, neither is life. A positive attitude about one's own abilities is necessary to endure the almost constant rejection that one experiences, directly and/or indirectly, on a daily basis during a career in the entertainment industry. Equally important, one must keep one's voice-over and acting career in the proper perspective . . . after all, it's only a job. Life (family, friends, health, etc.) is so much more important."

~ DORIAN HAREWOOD, best known as Simon Alexander Haley in the critically acclaimed television mini-series *Roots: The Next Generation*. His voice-over credits include being the voice of PBS.

"Every actor willingly or unwittingly signs on for one of the wildest thrill rides life can dish out. A career, complete with the highest highs and the lowest lows. The price of admission is uncertainty, insecurity and—all too often—unemployment. In my thirty years as a full-time voice actor, I've known all three. But the work, the work, the work—*always cures everything*. So, when the jobs are few and my positive attitude is waning, I find comfort in repeating to myself this simple—but reassuring mantra: 'I've worked in the past. I'll work in the future!' "

~ HARLAN HOGAN, is the author of the bestseller *VO: Tales and Techniques of a Voice-Over Actor*. His voice-over credits include Life® cereal.

"You want to know how a positive attitude has helped my career? It's simple. How many people with negative attitudes do you want to associate with? Well, the same goes for the people who are in the position to give you work. Negativity breeds negativity. It also defeats just about every purpose except suicide. A positive attitude can get a person through the worst of situations, including rejection, which is very common in this business. I know a colleague—a man with talent, experience, and good chops. But his attitude sucks! Consequently, he is out of work just about all of the time. Nobody wants to associate with him and his sob stories and depressing personality. It comes down to this: negativity and positivity are both self-reproducing conditions. That should make the choice between them reasonably easy to make."

~ DON LAFONTAINE, best known in the industry as the "King of Movie Trailers." He has voiced over 4,000 trailers.

"For me, a positive attitude is the only way to deal with the instability and rejection inherent in a career as a performer. A sense of self-confidence and a love of the work provide an anchor to keep you steady in an industry where uncertainty is the norm."

~ PHIL LAMARR, best known as a cast member of Fox's critically acclaimed "Mad TV." His voice-over credits include the voice of Hermes Conrad in the animated series *Futurama*.

"There are three definitive attributes that, I believe, have helped me become successful (by which I mean earn a living) in the voice-over business. First, is the burning desire to get into the business that I found extremely motivational and caused me to try various methods to 'get there.'

"Second, was being positively confident that I possessed the talent, training, and experience to do the job.

"The third is an outgoing positive and friendly attitude. Projecting such an attitude really helps to get through the hard times of the voice-over industry (being between jobs, losing auditions to other, perhaps, less talented persons, etc.).

"I, luckily, have the ability to look at the bright side of people and life. To realize, during the bad times, that there has to be an 'up' for there to be a 'down' and that if you're down now, then you'll soon be up. Life is a cyclical roller coaster ride. It is fraught with ups and downs. Putting out a positive attitude will make others feel positive about you.

"If you make others feel positive, they'll want you around them (this goes for producers with whom you've come into contact with as well as the common man)."

~ BURTON RICHARDSON, best known as the
announcer voice for *Family Feud* and
the *Arsenio Hall Show*.

"A positive attitude has helped me a great deal in my career; primarily because it has allowed me to keep 'Showbiz' in perspective. I grew up in Flint, Michigan, where, if you're lucky enough to have a job, you're probably hanging fenders on a Regal. An honorable profession to be sure; but not my cuppa Joe. Anytime "The Biz' starts to get to me, I remind myself that nobody ever held a gun to my head and forced me to be an actor. So, all that has happened to me as a result of being a performer, good and not so good, has been because of my choice. I'm living my dream and it's my responsibility. I mean, come on, I get paid U.S. dollars to do what used to get me in trouble in 7th grade by folks I would choose to be my friends. What more can one ask for?"

~ ROB PAULSEN, best known as the voice of the
boisterous and energetic laboratory mouse Pinky
on two hit series *Pinky and the Brain* and *Pinky,
Elmyra, and the Brain*.

"Patience, perseverance, and FAITH."

~ KEVIN MICHAEL RICHARDSON, best known as the
voice of The Joker in the animated
series *The Batman* and the smiley-
face price buster for Wal-Mart.

"Success in the voice business is based on the number of jobs you get; thus one must keep trying to get hired over and over again, which can be rough. So, I try to think positive and remember the law of rejection: 'You will be doing well if you land one session for every ten interviews or jobs you read for.' This can be devastating for the weak of heart. You must have faith in your talent, keep a positive attitude, and realize that is just the way it is and enjoy the challenge. I always like to look at the readings and interviews as going to work and the actual job as the coffee break.

~ FRANK WELKER, best known as the voice of Scooby Doo, from the animated television series, *Scooby Doo*, and the voice of Goddard in *The Adventures of Jimmy Neutron* animated series.

Afterword

RELY ON YOUR INTUITION TO KNOW WHEN THE TIME is right to take the next step toward enriching your life and elevating your voice-over career. When you make that decision, do it with confidence and pride—for you have committed to the challenge.

Glossary

Abundance—An overflow of wealth.

Affirmation—A declaration or statement about a positive action or actions you want to take place in your life.

Brainstorming—The unrestrained offering of ideas from a group to seek a solution.

Bring pack—A bag of positive affirmations to combat and deflect negative words and actions.

Butterflies—A nervous energy that is brought on by a sense of fear and anxiety.

Collaborative—Two or more people working on a project together with one common goal.

Comfort zone—Your most comfortable state at whatever you are presently doing.

Constitution—Your foundation and structure; your core.

Copywriter—A writer of copy for scripts or advertising.

Curmudgeon—A crusty, ill-tempered, and usually old man.

Cyber media—Computer-generated news.

Cyberspace—A complex electronic system; the Internet.

Diplomat—A tactful person.

Empower—To give power to someone; to authorize.

Empowerment cards—Cards with positive daily affirmations and illustrations on them.

Falsetto—An artificial way of singing in which the voice is much higher pitched than normal.

Fortify—To strengthen physically and emotionally.

Frame of mind—Your state of mind; how you feel generally at any given time.

Happenstance—Chance or accidental happening.

High five—A positive hand slap or pressing of the palms with another individual.

Infighting—Personal conflict within a group.

Inner spirit—What goes on inside your body and soul.

Inner voices—The negative versus positive energy within.

Interactive exercises—You actually touch the page with your index finger to participate in this exercise.

Interpersonal skills—Your ability to converse and interact with people who are in close physical proximity to you. There are many sensory channels used, and feedback is immediate.

Interpretation—To give one's own conception of an account or a script's copy.

Karma—The totality of one's acts. affects his or her future.

Mental warfare—The inner battle between negative and positive forces within your psyche.

Minoriteam—A cartoon series during the Cartoon Network's Adult Swim programming.

Mirror exercise—Conversations and affirmations to oneself while looking in the mirror.

Morph—Transforming into the persona of another person.

Multi-task—Do more than one thing at a time.

Natural voice—Your real-person, natural sound that you can dial up on request.

Negative buys—Purchases that sabotage your business.

Phat—An urban slang used to describe something as cool, great, or excellent.

Positive buys—Purchases that grow your business.

Positive foundation—A group of solid principles that your confidence is built on.

Positive realm—An upbeat, optimistic area.

Procrastinators—People who put off doing something and sometimes never do what they intended to do.

Prosperity—Wealth.

Paramount—Something that ranks high in importance to you.

Realist—A practical person; a down-to-earth person.

Rival friends—So-called friends who are secretly competitive with you.

Sound alike—To sound like another person to perfection; to mimic.

Tele-class—A class that is taught over the telephone on a teleconference phone line.

Telecommunications—The sharing of information by way of telephone systems.

Voice-over nutrients—Positive concepts and practices that feed your positive needs.

Bibliography & References

Alburger, James. *The Art of Voice Acting: The Craft and Business of Performing for Voice-Over.* Focal Press, 1998.

Baker, Joan. *Secrets of Voice-Over Success: Top Voice-Over Actors Reveal How They Did It.* Sentient Publications, 2005.

Berkley, Susan. *Speak to Influence: How to Unlock the Hidden Power of Your Voice.* Campbell Hall Press, 2nd ed., 2004.

Blanchard, Ken and Miller, Mark. *The Secret: What Great Leaders Know and Do.* Berrett-Koehler Publishers, 2004.

Cartwright, Nancy. *My Life As a Ten-Year-Old Boy.* Hyperion, 2001.

Cronauer, Adrian. *How to Read Copy: Professionals Guide to Delivering Voice-Overs and Broadcast Commercials.* Bonus Books, 1990.

Fisher, Jeffrey P. and Hogan, Harlan. *The Voice Actor's Guide to Home Recording.* Artistpro, 2005.

Merlin, Joanna. *Auditioning: An Actor Friendly Guide.* Vintage, 2001.

POPULAR SELF-HELP BOOKS

Britten, Rhonda. *Fearless Living.* Perigee Trade, 2002.

Cudney, Milton R. and Harry, Robert E. *Self-Defeating Behaviors: Free Yourself From the Habits, Compulsions, Feelings, and Attitudes That Hold You Back.* Harper San Francisco, 1999.

Goulston, Mark and Goldberg, Philip. *Get Out of Your Own Way; Overcoming Self-Defeating Behavior.* Pedigree Trade, 1996.

Kahn, Adam. *Self-Help Stuff that Works*, YouMe Works, 1999.

Pinkins, Tonya. *Get Over Yourself: How to Drop the Drama and Claim the Life You Deserve.* Hyperion, 2006.

Robbins, Anthony. *Unlimited Power: The New Science of Personal Achievement.* Free Press, 1997.

Smiley, Tavis. *Never Mind Success—Go For Greatness!: The Best Advice I Ever Received.* Hay House, 2006.

About Tomdor Publishing

Tomdor Publishing is an independent publisher of books and other publications that promote various categories in the entertainment industry, such as Voice-Overs, Music, Acting, Self-Help, and Self-Motivation.

Founded in 2003, this company has touched the lives of thousands of people who have expressed their appreciation through book sales, e-mailed letters, and faxes. Many careers have started and others have continued to grow from reading our books and taking our courses.

The goal of this company is to educate and motivate people to better themselves and be compelled to help others. We are dedicated to producing books and training that take advantage of the new adventures and opportunities available to the masses around the globe.

Other Available Products From Tomdor Publishing:

Step up to the Mic; A Positive Approach to Succeeding in Voice-Overs, Audio Book CD. 2007.

You Can Bank on Your Voice; Your Guide to a Successful Career in Voice-Overs, Paperback book. 2004. ISBN 0-9747678-0-8.

You Can Bank on Your Voice; Your Guide to a Successful Career in Voice-Overs, Audio book CD. 2004.

You can purchase these items at: **www.tomdorpublishing.com**

I Want to Hear From You

I want you to tell me a positive story from your life; an uplifting testimonial about how a positive attitude made your life easier.

Please let me know how your voice-over career has flourished since you decided to release yourself to the power of a positive attitude.

Your correspondence can be as long as you need it to be—flesh out the details about a positive thing that has occurred in the workplace for you. I will read every word of your letter and respond.

Share your experience. Hopefully this book has inspired you and stirred up a positive past event that has faded into a distant memory. Bring it out of the past and let it brighten up your present.

I look forward to hearing from you. Please send your positive stories to:

Tomdor Publishing
P.O. Box 1735
Agoura Hills, CA 91376

How to
Contact the Author

Agency Representation:
William Morris Agency
151 El Camino Drive
Beverly Hills, CA 90212
(310) 859-4085
www.wma.com

Tomdor Publishing
P.O. Box 1735
Agoura Hills, CA 91376-1735
(818) 207-2682
www.tomdorpublishing.com

Internet Contacts:
E-mail:
rodtalks@rodneysaulsberry.com or
rodtalks@aol.com

Website:
www.rodneysaulsberry.com or
www.alvoice.com